SO-CQS-666

The City of Chester

The Arms of Chester City Council

ABOVE: *The 14th-century Old Dee Bridge was, until 1832, the only bridge across the Dee at Chester into Wales.*

FRONT COVER: *Bridge Street, a fine example of Chester's unique feature 'the Rows'.*

BACK COVER: *The Eastgate. The present gate was built in 1769; the clock commemorates Queen Victoria's Diamond Jubilee.*

THE CITY OF CHESTER

THE ANCIENT ROMAN FORTRESS OF DEVA

IN AD 43 four Roman legions and auxiliary troops landed in Kent and so began the Roman occupation of Britain that was to last for more than 300 years. As the frontiers of the new province of the Roman empire were pushed northwards and the local tribes subdued, forts and roads were built in the wake of the advancing troops, but it was not until the second half of the 1st century that the Romans were able to begin the building of the fortress on the Dee, which they named Deva.

The site selected was ideal for military purposes. It was at the head of the tidal estuary of the river so that sea-going ships could anchor almost under the fortress walls and, at the same time, it was the lowest part of the river where it was feasible to build a bridge or construct a ford-crossing. There was a convenient sandstone plateau with command of the neighbouring countryside on which to build, and ample supplies of easily worked stone close at hand. So

★

far as immediate defence was concerned, the Dee formed an L-shaped bend here, so by siting the fortress in the inner angle of this it could be protected on its southern and western sides by a natural moat.

It was from about the late fifties of the 1st century that the legions began the construction in earth and timber of the future city of Chester. Of 'playing-card shape', that is a rectangle with rounded corners, it was about 450 yards from east to west and 650 yards from north to south, enclosing almost 60 acres within its walls. There were four gates, one in each side, and from these gates four main streets led to the central area of the fortress where the *principia*, or headquarters of the legion, stood. In modern Chester this site is now occupied partly

FACING PAGE, ABOVE: *The Bishop's House, Abbey Square, is a gracious 18th-century residence. The King's School, now on the Wrexham Road, once occupied the 19th-century buildings on the south side, now a bank.*

FACING PAGE, BELOW: *Abbey Square contains many fine examples of 18th-century architecture; these charming little houses are next to the abbey's refectory.*

RIGHT: *The 14th-century gateway to the old abbey has a good vaulted roof and made-up doors in either wall. Doubtless one would have led to a porter's lodge and the other perhaps to the almonry, where gifts were distributed to the poor. The abbey gate was an important feature of medieval Chester; at this spot each June a great fair was held on the feast of St Werburgh, and at Whitsuntide religious mystery plays were acted here. The gateway leads to the Town Hall Square and Northgate Street.*

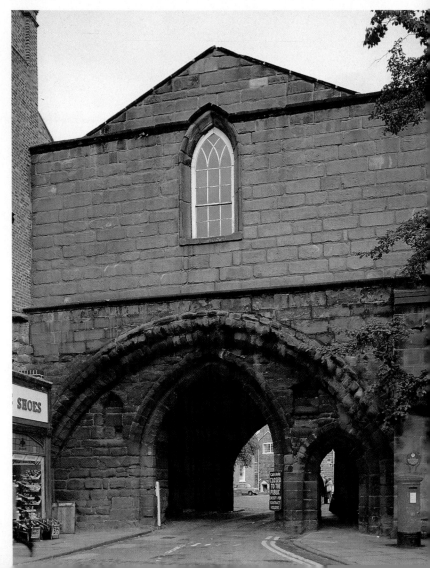

3

ABOVE: *View of the cathedral from the city walls, showing the south-east angle of the building. Extensively restored in the 19th century, it was originally a Benedictine abbey founded by the Norman earl Hugh Lupus and became a cathedral on the dissolution of the monasteries. Some Norman features remain, but the architecture spans the 12th to 19th centuries. Interesting points include the exquisite little 'Cobweb' picture, the mosaics (1883–86) on the north wall of the nave, and the Consistory Court.*

FAR LEFT: *The dean's stall, formerly the abbot's stall, on which is a tree of Jesse surmounted by the coronation of Our Lady.*

LEFT: *The vice-dean's stall, showing the pelican in her piety. The stalls and misericords are beautifully made; the carvings include an elephant and castle and a humorous one depicting an old monk with the Devil tipping up his tankard.*

by St Peter's church at the Cross, and the principal streets of the city—Eastgate, Northgate, Watergate and Bridge Streets—still meet here almost 1,900 years after a Roman surveyor marked them out.

Although the first fortress of earthen ramparts enclosing wooden buildings was rude and primitive, considerable reconstruction in stone took place as the years of occupation went by, and eventually Deva must have been an impressive legionary headquarters with its huge *principia*, governor's and officers' houses, baths, clubs, perhaps a temple and theatre, granaries and barracks all within the massive walls over 20 feet high, and with a civil settlement and an 8,000-seat amphitheatre outside.

The date when the XX Legion withdrew from Deva is uncertain, but it was probably about the middle of the 4th century and there followed a period of 500 years—the Dark Ages—when little is known about the fortress except that it fell into desolation and decay as it was ravaged in turn by warring Britons, Scots, Northumbrians and Danes. Not until the 9th century does the picture clear a little, when it is known that the body of the Saxon saint Werburgh was brought from Staffordshire to Chester for protection from the Danes, so it would appear that the Saxons must have been firmly established in the city about that time. The *Anglo-Saxon Chronicle* records that in 907 Legeceaster (i.e. the city of the legions) was new made, and this was done by Aethelflaed, a daughter of Alfred the Great, who was known as the Lady of the Mercians. She restored the fortress, rebuilding and extending the walls, and raised a castle on ground near the river, outside the former Roman defences. From this time until the Norman conquest, Chester recovered some of its former glory and about the year 972 the Saxon king

Continued on page 8

★

ABOVE RIGHT: *This beautiful window (1961) above the great west door of the cathedral shows Our Lady and northern saints.*

RIGHT: *The south-east corner of the cathedral precincts now contains a free-standing bell-tower opened by HRH the Duke of Gloucester in June 1975. In the foreground is the Memorial Garden to the Cheshire Regiment. There is a small Cheshire Regiment Chapel, with regimental colours, in the cathedral.*

ABOVE: *Near the Newgate, the walls overlook the Nine Houses. Of the nine timber-framed 17th-century houses, six remain. They were restored in 1969. Nearby are the Wishing Steps and the Recorder's Steps.*

LEFT: *The canal winds towards the Northgate Lock, with King Charles' Tower in the background. At the north-east angle of the Roman fortress, the tower derives its name from the tradition that here Charles I watched the rout of his forces by Parliamentary troops after the battle of Rowton Moor in 1645. Previously it was known as the Newton Tower, as it overlooked the township of that name; later as the Phoenix Tower from the badge above the door, that of the Painters', Glaziers', Stationers' and Embroiderers' Company or Guild, which used it as a meeting place. Containing mementoes of the Civil War, it is open to the public during the summer, when the horse-drawn barge takes visitors past the tower on its trips, including one to the zoo.*

ABOVE: *The previous Town Hall having been destroyed by fire, the Council held a competition to select a design for a new building. This was won by W. H. Lynn of Belfast. The Gothic-style structure has a central tower 160 feet high. Costing £40,000, it was opened by the Prince of Wales (later Edward VII) in 1869. Some of the rooms open to the public include the Assembly Room (containing fine portraits of the Grosvenor family), where free concerts are held from September to March on Tuesdays at lunchtime, and the Council Chamber. On application to the city archivist, the Muniment Room, containing the ancient charters and other documents, the 15th-century great sword of Chester and the city mace, may be inspected. Much of the civic plate is now at the Grosvenor Museum. Less than ten minutes' walk away, near the Fountains Roundabout, is the Northgate Arena, where amenities include an ultra-modern swimming-pool, saunas, bar and concert/conference hall seating approximately 1,600. Also nearby is the new Library and the Market.*

Edgar, according to tradition, was rowed in state on the River Dee from his palace to St John's church, the oarsmen being minor kings from Wales, Ireland, the Isle of Man and elsewhere who had come to swear allegiance to him.

Chester is reputed to have been the last of the important towns of Saxon England to have fallen to the Norman invaders and it was not until 1070, four years after the battle of Hastings, that Cheshire was subdued and the town once more laid waste. In 1071 the earldom of Chester was created and, after it had been held for a few months by Gherbod, a Fleming, the first of a line of Norman earls was Hugh d'Avranches, a nephew of William the Conqueror, who became known as Hugh Lupus —Hugh the Wolf—presumably because of his rapacity. And yet it was Earl Hugh who persuaded Anselm, abbot of Bec in Normandy, to come to Chester to help him to refound the church of St Werburgh as a great Benedictine abbey. Anselm became Archbishop of Canterbury in 1093 and was later canonised.

There were eight Norman earls of Chester and for 166 years they ruled by the sword a palatinate that was virtually an independent kingdom and which had its own parliament, laws, taxes, courts of justice, nobility and army. These earls were Hugh, Richard, Ranulph le Meschin, Ranulph de Gernon, Hugh of Kevelioc, Ranulph de Blundeville (the

★

FACING PAGE: *The Cross (containing some pieces of the original High Cross) was restored to its original position outside St Peter's church in 1975, as a contribution to European Architectural Heritage Year, by the Chester Civic Trust and the Department of the Environment. St Peter's church, one of the principal city churches, stands on part of the site of the headquarters of the Roman fortress. An old custom was to hang a large glove outside the church 14 days before the Chester Fairs and during the July and October fairs. St Peter's is now used by the Freemen and Guilds, but Holy Communion and Sunday matins are also held here. The church is also a Christian centre for lectures, exhibitions and concerts.*

RIGHT: *The Water Tower. Before the waters of the Dee receded, this sandstone tower, built about 1325, assisted in guarding the port of Chester. It projects from the north-west angle of the walls and is connected to them by a massive spur wall.*

9

most powerful of the earls, who reigned for 50 years and had great influence throughout England) and John le Scot. John died in 1237, leaving as his heirs three sisters and two nieces, whereupon Henry III annexed the earldom to the Crown 'lest so fair a dominion should be divided among women'. The king conferred the earldom on his son, later Edward I, and for 700 years it has remained an apanage of the eldest son of the reigning monarch, except for 1264–65 when the earldom was held by Simon de Montfort.

The period of the Norman earls, 1071–1237, was a turbulent one in Chester, as the city was used as a base for warlike expeditions against the Welsh and the Irish, and even crusaders were recruited here. Fire swept through the wooden buildings of the town from time to time and much of it was burned down in the great fires of 1140 and 1180, whilst in 1227 the bridge over the Dee was destroyed by floods, thus cutting the main road into north Wales. However, despite the troubled times, with savage fighting, natural disasters, rough justice with sentences ranging from decapitation or hanging and quartering to the pillory and stocks, the inhabitants continued to survive and even flourish as merchants and tradesmen, and Chester became the most important port on the north-west coast.

From Roman times, sea-going vessels had used the estuary of the Dee and anchored under the walls of Chester. The Danes had sailed up the river, founding communities in Wirral and even occupying the ruins of Chester itself when hotly pursued by the Saxons. King Edgar the Peaceable had sailed with a great fleet from the Severn to the Dee and so to Chester. From the 12th to the 14th centuries the port enjoyed its most prosperous period, especially in trading with Ireland, and there were considerable imports of all kinds of fish, hides and skins, Irish wool and linen, French wines, Spanish ironware, fruits and spices, grain and cloth. Ships sailing from Chester carried cheese and salt, gloves and candles. The mayor of Chester exercised considerable authority over the use of the estuary and even today bears the title of 'Admiral of the Dee'. Up to the end of the 16th century Liverpool was looked upon by Cestrians as being 'but a creek of the port of Chester'.

Unfortunately, during the 15th century the estuary began to silt up, and instead of merchant ships tying up by the Water Gate at the foot of Watergate

Street, they were forced to anchor some 12 miles downstream. As a result, and despite frantic efforts to provide new havens nearer to Chester, the trade of the port declined and there was great distress in the city, so much so that royal taxation (the fee farm) on Chester was reduced successively from £100 to £50 to £30, and finally to £20.

In 1506 Henry VII granted to Chester its Great Charter which, amongst other things, constituted the city a county, and up to 1974, when reorganisation of local government took place, official announcements were headed 'The City and County of the City of Chester'. The title now is 'The Council of the City of Chester'. Life during the 16th and 17th centuries, although not without its dangers, had some compensations, the citizens enjoying their fairs and games, performances of the mystery plays, horse racing on the Roodee, football, archery and bowling, while more blood-thirsty sports were bull- and bear-baiting and cock-fighting.

The mystery plays (so called because these religious plays were performed by the craft guilds or mysteries) were of

Continued on page 14

★

FACING PAGE, ABOVE: *Close to the Roman amphitheatre (the largest yet uncovered in Britain) is the Newgate, and also the peaceful Roman Garden. The Newgate, displaying the arms of the city, of the Grosvenor, Stanley and Egerton families, and of the Prince of Wales (who is also Earl of Chester), was built in 1938—the former gate being too narrow for modern traffic. The Roman Garden contains Roman remains found in the city, including a hypocaust.*

FACING PAGE, BELOW: *Bonewaldesthorne's Tower stands at the north-west angle of the walls and its name has long puzzled antiquaries. One suggestion is that it is named after an Anglo-Saxon thane; another theory is that the B is a mistake for TH and the name is derived from the Norse, the tower having overlooked the meeting place of a Norse 'Thing' or parliament.*

RIGHT: *The Goblin Tower, an oddly shaped half-tower on the north wall, has borne the nickname of 'Pemberton's Parlour' for the past 200 years, for John Pemberton, a rope-maker and mayor of Chester in 1730, used it as a vantage-point from which to watch his men on the rope-walk below. An earlier name was Dille's Tower.*

FACING PAGE: *St John the Baptist's church, which celebrated its 900th anniversary in 1975, was Chester's cathedral in Mercian times until the see moved to Lichfield, so Chester can lay claim to having two cathedrals. The ruins are of the 12th-century choir. The present church contains splendid Norman arches. The St John's Festival Orchestra provides concerts during the year, and there are lunchtime concerts in the summer.*

ABOVE: *The Anchorite's Cell is an 18th-century building with some medieval stonework. It is a particularly peaceful spot close to Grosvenor Park and the Groves.*

RIGHT: *The Grosvenor Park was a gift from the 2nd Marquis of Westminster in 1867. The lovely, well-kept flower-beds and shady trees provide Cestrian and visitor alike with a pleasing retreat. Chester has several times won the BTA 'Britain in Bloom' award for the North-West.*

some importance in the life of the city and large sums of money were spent in staging them each year. They were also known as the 'Whitsun plays' as they took place during three days of Whitsun week, nine on Monday, nine on Tuesday and six or seven on Wednesday. It is likely that these plays originated from a desire to make the Latin teaching of the Church more intelligible to the people, and all were based on the Bible. Each city company undertook responsibility for staging a play, and the allocation was not without appropriateness: for example the story of the Flood was performed by the Water-drawers of Dee; the Last Supper by the Bakers, and so on.

Each play was mounted on a large, two-tiered waggon, the lower part being used as a dressing-room, the upper as the stage. The first performance of the first play of the day was given at the abbey gateway, and from there the waggons would be drawn through the town, stopping at regular stations for further performances, so that the spectators, by remaining at one spot, would see a succession of plays performed before them.

There are, of course, several cycles of mystery plays, but that of Chester is believed to be the oldest, dating from about 1375 and preceding other cycles at York, Coventry and other towns by several years. They continued to be performed regularly for 200 years until 1575, when they were suppressed by authority as being 'popish plaies'. Some of the plays have been revived in recent years, sponsored by the Chester City Council, and revised versions presented in the cathedral precincts and at the Cross.

Reference to the cathedral reminds us that although trade had its ups and downs, the religious life of the city seems on the whole to have prospered under the protection of the Norman earls and later the reigning monarchs, for churches, friaries and nunneries abounded.

Tradition has it that a Christian church stood on the site of the present cathedral even in Roman times, but the history of any pre-Conquest building is largely a matter of conjecture and we can be certain only of the development that took place from the time of Earl Hugh Lupus onwards.

The relics of St Werburgh were moved from Hanbury in Staffordshire to Chester, probably in the year 875, at a time when the Danes were invading Mercia. When Aethelflaed restored the ruined city and extended its boundaries in 907 it is likely that she would have devoted attention to the church of St Werburgh at the same time. Domesday Book states that the church had 13 houses—'one is the warden's the others the canons'.'

After the Conquest, Earl Hugh sent to Bec in Normandy to ask Anselm, abbot of the Benedictine monastery there, to advise him on the founding of a similar community in Chester. Together, the earl and the abbot established the new abbey and traces of their work may still be seen in the cathedral, mainly in the north transept. A little later in date are the undercroft and the nave of St Anselm's chapel, which were followed by the chapter house, parlour and refectory, possibly occasioned by an increase in the number of monks to 40.

Succeeding centuries saw the growth of the abbey continue until Henry VIII dissolved the monasteries and, in 1541, the abbey church became the cathedral church of the new diocese of Chester, and the last abbot became the first dean of the cathedral.

From time to time the townsfolk and clergy clashed and it is recorded that

Continued on page 16

FACING PAGE, LEFT: *Bishop Lloyd's house in Watergate Street Row is a splendid example of a 17th-century town house. Although named after Dr George Lloyd (1560–1615), who was bishop of Chester (1604–15), it is unlikely that he used it as an episcopal residence. The frontage bears a number of richly carved panels depicting biblical scenes, animals and coats of arms. The bishop's eldest daughter, Anne, married first Thomas Yale, grandfather of Elihu Yale, after whom Yale University is named, and secondly Theophilus Eaton, who was the governor of New Haven, in Connecticut, from 1639 until 1658.*

FACING PAGE, RIGHT: *Tudor House in Lower Bridge Street is reputed to be the oldest house in Chester. It has been beautifully restored over recent years. A contrast in architectural styles is provided by the graceful terrace of Georgian houses further down the street, near the Bridgegate.*

ABOVE: *Chester has long been famous for its unique feature, the Rows, to be found on both sides of Eastgate, Bridge and Watergate Streets. The Watergate Street Rows are the oldest and particularly fascinating. In two tiers are to be found the shops of wine-merchants (with a superb 13th-century crypt), jewellers, goldsmiths and silversmiths, together with shops selling gowns, shoes, toys and a wide range of antiques and other merchandise. The Rows provide ideal shopping conditions, regardless of the weather, while the modern shopping precincts also have much to offer. The Eastgate Street and Bridge Street Rows are both now linked to the modern Grosvenor shopping precinct, which houses a collection of shops selling clothes, furniture, fine china and crystal, books and many other attractive and useful commodities, as well as restaurants. There is also direct access to the walls from the precinct, and two National Car Parks nearby.*

there was a riot in the abbey in 1393 when severe destruction was caused. In 1607, a canon of the cathedral challenged the ancient right of the mayor to enter the cathedral preceded by the great civic sword carried point uppermost. Shortly afterwards the sword-bearer died and when his corpse was carried to the cathedral for burial, attended by the mayor and council, the prebendary caused the west doors of the cathedral to be shut against them. Nothing daunted, the mayor and his party gained entrance by another door and marched to their usual place in the choir with the sword borne before them, and the body was eventually brought in. These incidents gave rise to considerable resentment in the town and legal action was taken to decide the issue. The two judges of assize who heard the case upheld the city's claim, and the right of the mayor and his sword-bearer to carry the civic sword, point up, in the cathedral is still observed.

The cathedral was extensively restored in the 19th century, with Sir Gilbert Scott as the architect.

One of the features for which Chester is so justly famous is its Rows, the arrangement of shops which line the principal streets at first-floor height. Once seen they are unlikely ever to be forgotten, but to describe them in words is not at all easy. At street level, or in many cases slightly below it so that one has to go down a short flight of steps to enter, are the ground-floor shops. Above these is a footway, or 'Row', flanked on one side by an open gallery overlooking the street, and on the other by more shops. The upper floors of the shops in the Row project over it, so as to form a ceiling, and the resulting covered walk, with most attractive shop-windows on one side, and a view over the busy pageant of the streets on the other, is unique.

Many theories have been advanced as to how the Rows came into being, some even ascribing them to Roman times, but a 14th-century origin seems more likely as the first mention of them by name occurs in the city records for the year 1331. The most plausible theory put forward is that from the 4th century onwards, when the legion withdrew, great mounds of stone and rubble from decaying and destroyed Roman buildings lined the main streets of the city, those now known as Bridge Street, Watergate Street, Eastgate Street and

ABOVE: *The name of the Roodee is derived from two Anglo-Saxon words, 'rood' meaning 'cross', and 'eye' meaning 'island', that is 'the island of the cross'. It was once the harbour of the Romans. Since 1540 horse races have been held here, and meetings now take place in May, June, July, August or September.*

FACING PAGE, ABOVE: *The River Dee flows through the tree-lined Groves, where band concerts are held on Sundays from May to September. Enjoyable river cruises commence from the Groves, while the visitor with a wish for strenuous exercise can hire a rowing boat. Regattas, a canoe slalom and raft race are also held on the river.*

FACING PAGE, BELOW: *The elegant Grosvenor Bridge over the Dee was built to the designs of Thomas Harrison (1744–1829), a noted Chester architect, and opened in 1832 by the young Princess Victoria, who became queen five years later. When it was built, the 200-foot span of the main arch was the greatest single span of any stone arch in the world and undoubtedly a remarkable example of engineering skill. It cost £50,000 to build. Glimpsed through the arch is the church of St Mary Without the Walls (1887).*

Continued on page 18

Northgate Street. In this connection it is significant that the continuity of the Rows does not extend beyond the line of the walls of the original Roman fortress. It is suggested, therefore, that the early shopkeepers would have put up stalls at street level, in front of the massive ruins, in order to cry their wares and that, in the course of time, more substantial merchants with an eye for a good trading site would have erected shops on top of the ruins and behind the stalls below. For the convenience of their customers, steps up to the shops would have been built and a footpath made joining the frontages. At this time the Rows would have been open to the sky, but as business expanded and the merchant required better accommodation for his family and to enhance his status, he would have built upper floors over his shop and, to make the best use of the space available, would have carried these over the Row so that they were level with the stalls on the street.

Whether or not this is the correct explanation of Chester's Rows is perhaps arguable, but no one who has used them could fail to agree that for wet-weather shopping and freedom from traffic hazards they are ideal. The busiest Rows are those on the south side of Eastgate Street and the east side of Bridge Street. The Rows in Watergate Street, particularly on the south side,

★

LEFT: *The Chester Heritage Centre, formerly St Michael's church, was opened in 1975, as part of Chester's European Architectural Heritage Year programme. An audio-visual presentation shows the architecture of the city and its conservation. Five minutes' walk away, near St John's church, is the Chester Visitor Centre, where there is a reconstruction of a Row as it might have been in Victorian times, also a tourist information centre and other attractions for visitors.*

FACING PAGE, ABOVE: *The Old King's Head is an interesting example of a half-timbered 17th-century house. This was once in the possession of the Randle Holme family, famous heralds and antiquaries of their day.*

FACING PAGE, BELOW: (left) *The Bear and Billet (1664), just inside the Bridgegate, was the town house of the Earls of Shrewsbury, and* (right) *the Falcon, another 17th-century building, at the top of Lower Bridge Street, was that of the Grosvenor family.*

19

are less sophisticated but most interesting and, moreover, pass by some fine old houses, such as Bishop Lloyd's house, displaying richly carved fronts.

Visitors to Chester with the time to spare should not omit from their itinerary a tour of the walls. This two-mile walk is unique in this country, as no other walled town has been able to preserve a continuous circuit as is the case in Chester. The views from the walls comprise a mixture of fine prospects and some not so fine, but the overall picture is full of interest.

The first walls were built by the Roman legions and consisted of turf ramparts surmounted by wooden palisading overlooking a ditch on the outside. As the centuries of occupation continued, stone walls and gateways gradually replaced the earth and timber structures until the fortress was ringed with massive stone defences. Parts of the Roman wall are to be seen between King Charles' Tower and the Northgate, while foundations of the south-east angle tower have been exposed by the Newgate.

The maintenance of the walls has always been of importance to the city, and in the past officials known as muragers were appointed to collect special taxes for their upkeep. Proposals to breach the walls with postern or other gates have always been strongly opposed and the abbot's gate to his kitchen-garden outside the eastern wall was a bone of contention between the town council and the abbey for many years.

The present circuit of the walls is, of course, greater in extent than the wall built by the Romans. If one stands on the Eastgate by the clock tower and looks westward along Eastgate Street, past St Peter's church at the Cross and down Watergate Street, as far as the spire of Holy Trinity church on the right (now the Guildhall, which houses a small collection of exhibits of the 23 city guilds), this view marks the width of the Roman fortress. The angle-towers were at the present King Charles' Tower (NE), Morgan's Mount (NW), near to the junction of Weaver Street and White Friars (SW) and by the Newgate (SE). Whether the extension of the walls down to the

river and including the castle was carried out in Saxon or medieval times has never been satisfactorily determined by local historians.

Chester Castle is disappointing for those who like to see keeps, moats and battlements, for these were largely done away with at the end of the 18th century to make way for Harrison's classical assize courts, gaol, barracks, armoury, and the regimental museum of the Cheshire Regiment, the whole fronted with a great Doric gateway. The oldest part of the castle proper is the 13th-century tower which houses the chapel of St Mary de Castro.

Famous historical names do not seem to have been associated with the castle at any time, apart from the fact that it held a royal prisoner in the person of Richard II, that James II attended mass in the chapel, and that John Wesley took refuge here when he met with much opposition in Chester. Other figures connected with it were in the main local. Throughout its existence its function has been more administrative than military.

From the 1st to the 17th centuries the history of Chester was both dramatic and colourful—Roman legions, Saxon kings and queens, Norman earls, Plantagenet and Tudor monarchs all trod its streets. Life was wild and dangerous but exciting. This period really came to an end in the 17th century, when the siege of Chester during the Civil War was the last event of any national significance in the annals of the city. Chester was a Royalist stronghold, as might be expected, and held out stoutly for Charles I against the Parliamentary troops. In September 1645 the king watched from the walls the rout of his cavalry following the battle of Rowton Moor, before making his own escape over the Old Dee Bridge into north Wales. The starved citizens held out for a further five months before capitulating.

With the return of peace, Chester settled down to rebuild its trade, while the merchants and county families built fine houses in the town in traditional black-and-white style. Quiet progress continued in the 18th and 19th cen-

FACING PAGE, LEFT: *The Cheshire Regiment Museum in Chester Castle is open throughout the year. The beautiful silver on display has some specially touching associations, while the uniforms and other exhibits provide an interesting collection of military memorabilia covering the Cheshire Regiment and the 5th Inniskilling Dragoon Guards.*

FACING PAGE, RIGHT: *The Fishergirl from Brittany (c. 1900) from the Toy Museum in Bridge Street Row.*

ABOVE AND RIGHT: *The present group of buildings known collectively as Chester Castle consists of a 13th-century tower; 19th-century buildings designed by Thomas Harrison to house new assize courts, gaol, barracks and armoury; and the new County Hall. Harrison's impressive Grand Entrance* (above) *was begun in 1811 and finished two years later in the classical Doric style. Agricola's Tower* (right), *despite its name, has no Roman connections. Built in the 13th century, this massive square tower is all that is left of the ancient castle.*

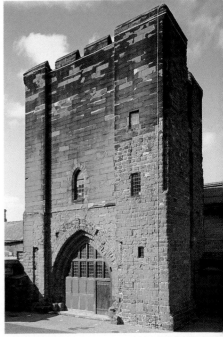

Continued on page 22

turies and only elections provided any excitement. The 19th century saw the arrival of the railways and Chester became an important junction, but fortunately the industrial revolution stayed away. Today Chester is a busy city, the gateway to North Wales and Wirral, a centre for government and local administration, noted for its shops and buildings and, above all, its atmosphere and the charm of its setting built up during 1,900 years of stirring existence.

With local government reorganisation in 1974 the old city and the former Chester and Tarvin Rural Districts were combined, forming the new district of Chester. The new district was granted a royal charter conferring borough status and the new borough was granted the title and dignity of a city and is known as the City of Chester. The county of Cheshire is now divided into eight districts – that of Chester covers 44,818 hectares, the population being 116,657.

Many picturesque villages, beauty spots and places of interest now come within the new City of Chester boundaries. Two and a half miles from the city centre, to the left of the A41, Whitchurch Road, lies the attractive village of Christleton. In 1645 the battle of Rowton Moor was fought nearby, King Charles I, from the Phoenix Tower, Chester (now known as King Charles' Tower), watching his unfortunate army defeated.

A few miles further along the A41 turn off left again to Beeston. High on a hill, commanding splendid views of the Cheshire plain and the Welsh hills,

stand the ruins of Beeston Castle. Destroyed by Cromwell, it is now gradually being rebuilt. The Sandstone Trail and Bickerton Hills nearby afford pleasant rambling and picnicking places.

Fourteen miles from Chester turn right off the A41 at Hampton for Malpas, one of Cheshire's oldest and most picturesque small towns. The superb 14th-century church of St Oswald is worthy of a visit. Bishop Heber, composer of many well-loved hymns, was born in Malpas. The famous Cheshire cheese is made at Overton Hall, a mile and a half away.

If the city is left via the Old Dee Bridge at Handbridge, one comes to Eccleston – a charming village mentioned in the Domesday Book. Here, in magnificent surroundings, is the residence of the Duke of Westminster. The gardens and Coach Museum are open to the public on Easter Sunday, the Spring Bank Holiday Sunday and a Sunday in July.

Other villages nearby are Farndon (famous for its strawberry fields) and Tarvin, where the Bruen Chapel in the lovely church commemorates the well-known Calvinistic Puritan, John Bruen, who lived at nearby Stapleford Hall. Barrow, with its field names and shapes, bears testimony to Anglo-Saxon times. At Backford, horrific gargoyles can be seen on the 16th-century Perpendicular-style tower. A short distance from the church is Chorlton Hall, where George Ormerod wrote his *History of Chester*. Here are but some of the many delightful and interesting places to visit when in Chester.

ABOVE: *Set in attractive gardens and administered by the North of England Zoological Society, Chester Zoo covers (with adjoining farm land) 333 acres at Upton, approximately 2½ miles from the city centre but easily reached by a frequent bus service. The zoo is open throughout the year and has good catering facilities.*

FACING PAGE, ABOVE: *The canal at Christleton. Many holidaymakers moor alongside the peaceful banks, while the horse-drawn barge trip through the locks is a popular tourist attraction. Three pack-horse bridges at Christleton formed part of the medieval Chester to London road.*

FACING PAGE, BELOW: *Farndon boasts a 14th-century bridge; drive over it and you are in Wales! In the church of St Chad is held a rush-bearing service on the second Sunday in July each year. Look out for the steeplejack's prayer on the belfry wall.*

ABOVE: *In Old Hall Street, Malpas, are some attractive old 'magpie' cottages near Malpas Cross, where on Boxing Day the crowds gather to watch the meet move off. The name Malpas is Norman, meaning 'bad road'. Due to their close proximity to Wales, Malpas and the surrounding countryside were constantly raided by the Welsh.*

RIGHT: *Malpas Church has several interesting features, including the fine 13th-century iron-bound chest made by a local blacksmith and the family vaults of the Cholmondeley and Brereton families. The nave ceiling has a magnificent array of carvings and bosses. Two windows of note have 16th- and 17th-century Flemish panels.*

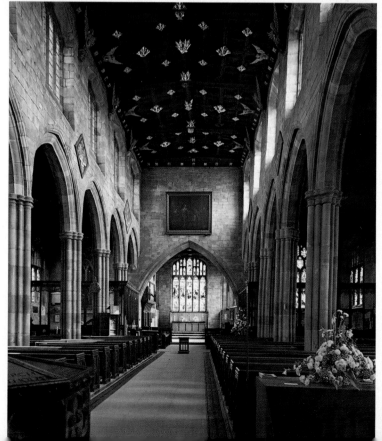

ACKNOWLEDGEMENTS
The publishers are grateful to the Chief Executive and Director of Finance, Chester City Council, for permission to reproduce the arms of the City of Chester on page 1, and to Cheshire County Council for the map on the inside front cover. The text is by E. H. Mason, former Deputy Director of Cheshire County Library and Museum Services and revised by Joan Houghton MBE, former Publicity Officer, Chester City Council. All the photographs are by Sydney W. Newbery, except those on the back cover and pages 3, 17 and 19 bottom left, by Andy Williams, p.14 left by Malcolm Osman/Woodmansterne, and p. 22, by P. A. Wait, Assistant Curator of Mammals and Birds, Chester Zoo.

ISBN 0 85372 229 3